Tired of Being Black

Tired *of* Being Black

RODNEY JORDAN

iUniverse, Inc.
Bloomington

Tired of Being Black

iUniverse books may be ordered through booksellers or by contacting:

iUniverse
1663 Liberty Drive
Bloomington, IN 47403
www.iuniverse.com
1-800-Authors (1-800-288-4677)

ISBN: 978-1-4759-4524-9 (sc)
ISBN: 978-1-4759-4525-6 (e)

Library of Congress Control Number: 2012915110

Printed in the United States of America

iUniverse rev. date: 09/07/2012

Table of Contents

Prelude

Tired of Being Black was written to raise awareness among blacks, but applies to other races as well. There are a number of issues, struggles, and stereotypes that plague the black population today. My goal is for people of all races, especially blacks, to evaluate their words, actions, and thoughts. When dealing with stereotypes, not everyone in a group fits the stereotype, but awareness and understanding can sometimes help us deal with others, unlike us, in a more positive manner.

There are times, when we as humans, judge others for many different reasons, race just happens to be a popular one. At other times, we provide ammunition for others to think wrongly of us or to form negative opinions about people affiliated with us. It is very easy to say they shouldn't, but if ten black guys live in a neighborhood and nine of them rob the neighborhood convenience store, it is fair to predict that the tenth guy is going to do it also.

I grew up as a troubled child in Norfolk, Virginia, during the eighties and nineties. I easily fell into many of the stereotypes associated with black males. I hated to read, stayed in the principal's office, and didn't really live up to my academic potential until my last two years of undergraduate school. I tried drugs, got into a few fights, and gave my mother a difficult time before she finally put me out, at the age of twelve. I used to let my pants sag and addressed my friends as "niggers." My parents didn't raise me that way; I just chose to be that way.

There were many people who positively influenced me, but Mr. Wilson, my tenth grade history teacher, saved my life. He taught me some valuable lessons that I still follow today. I remember being seven tenths of a point short of earning a D during our first interim grading period. I asked him to give me that fraction of a point so that I would have a passing grade. He said, "If you want anything in this class, you will earn it." Because I was determined to show him I was really capable of meeting his standards, I finished his class with an A. He challenged me to be a better student and a better individual as I neared manhood. Mr. Wilson refused to cut me any slack or allow me to do, say, and think as I had before meeting him. He didn't force me to do anything, yet he educated me, clarified things, and let me decide for myself, knowing the consequences and rewards.

In this literary work, I present my point of view based on my personal experiences, experiences of my family and friends, and observations I've made from watching television and listening to the radio. My hope is that readers will first reflect on their own lives, and then think about others they know. I know there are successful, respected, and honorable black people—both past and present—but it wouldn't hurt to have a few more.

Chapter 1

Name Calling

I'm tired of being black.

I'm tired of calling other black guys niggers.

I'm tired of them calling me a nigger.

Do any of us know where that word comes from?

Do we know the true meaning of the word?

We call each other niggers and it's okay,

but let a white person call us a nigger

and we're ready to fight, kill, or start a riot.

I wonder how Martin Luther King would feel

if someone

addressed him by saying,

"What's up my nigger?"

I doubt he would ever call someone a nigger.

We took a word

that was used to degrade our ancestors and

made it a personal greeting.

Our ancestors

were spit on, beaten, and raped

while being called derogatory names.

They were viewed as worthless beings—

not even referred to as humans.

They were only good enough

for hard labor or

childbearing and caretaking.

Is that what we are saying about each other

when we call each other niggers?

Maybe we're special niggers

because we greet each other with the word,

followed by a handshake, chest bump, and

a grin?

I'm tired of other black people calling me a sellout

just because I matured

and moved beyond the stereotypes that black men

are either no-good fathers, criminals,

or drug abusers.

I saw my life and my parents' lives, and

knew that I could have more;

knew that I could be more successful

than they were, regardless of how

little or much they had.

I'm tired of calling other black people sellouts

just because they didn't grow up in crime-infested and

drug-infested neighborhoods

like I did.

Why are they wrong because their parents went to

college and

became successful in medicine, law, or business?

Why should they walk around feeling ashamed

because they were able to eat dinner as a family,

and discuss the good and bad highlights of their day?

They have nothing to feel badly about.

They didn't get to choose their parents.

They were born into a family,

just like I was.

The fact that their parents own a gorgeous house,

drive luxury cars, take them on vacations every year,

attend their sporting events and other

extracurricular activities, and promote respect in their

homes,

doesn't make them any less black than me,

nor does it make them sellouts.

I'm tired of other races trying to figure out what to call me.

"Do you prefer African American or Black?"

Let's see, when other races

didn't care about my race, we were...

coons, niggers, fuzzies, jigaboos, negros

porch monkeys, tar babies, and colored.

Those that hated us

found any and every word they could to

break us down.

Now, because of wars, protests, boycotts, riots,

and other movements,

they want to know if I prefer to be called

Black or African American.

Why not identify me

by the name my parents gave me?

I don't hear the confusion

when other races are being identified.

I have never heard anyone

ask a white person, if they preferred to be called

White or European American.

I'm tired of hearing about

how my skin color doesn't matter.

If it doesn't matter,

why do I have to check black

on every application I complete?

People want to know my skin color

before I can get a scholarship, a job,

an education, a car, or a house.

Stop feeding me this garbage

that colleges and universities,

companies and businesses,

government officials and politicians,

are just trying to be fair—

that's the reason for wanting to know

whether I'm black or not.

They need to have a certain number of minorities

within their organization,

in order to receive funding from various sources.

They are then able to manipulate

how much of it

will actually be used to benefit

the minority population,

their majority population, and

how much they are going to keep

for themselves.

Chapter 2

That Time of Year

I'm tired of celebrating "Black History Month."

What is the point of making such a big deal

about black accomplishments, twenty-eight days a year?

White achievements

are built into our everyday lives.

When we open textbooks in schools,

white history is in there, but

they don't have their own month.

I'm tired of hearing black people say,

"well, they have the other eleven months."

No they don't, they have all twelve!

No one tells them

when or how to appreciate their heritage.

They don't focus on what happened in the past,

they spend their time trying to make things happen

for today and tomorrow.

On top of all of that,

we get the shortest month of the year and

we are okay with it, proud of it, and

acknowledge it.

No one should tell us

when or how to celebrate our heritage,

our accomplishments,

or anything else pertaining to our race.

We should do it willingly,

on our own, and on a regular basis.

Chapter 3

Special Privileges

I'm tired of getting certain privileges,

benefits, and opportunities

just because I'm black.

So what?

I don't need any extra bonuses in life

because of my skin color.

If someone is going to pay for me to attend college

it should be

because I earned it,

not because I'm black.

It's not okay for scholarships to be offered to me

because of my skin color, but

denied to other students for the same reason.

There are no advantages in schools anymore

thanks to integration.

We all sit in the same classrooms, use the same

resources,

and are taught by the same teachers.

I, as a black student, have the same opportunities,

as the other students.

As long as people feel they have to isolate me,

do extra things for me, or

only offer certain opportunities to me,

because I'm black,

it shows that blacks

have not been

accepted into mainstream America.

I don't know of any black people

who would be okay with

majority scholarships

for white students.

Therefore, we as blacks shouldn't accept minority
scholarships.
Also, isn't it just as much of a slap in the face
for someone to give me an avenue
on the basis of my skin color,
as it is for them to directly tell me I can't do it
because I'm black?

If I set reachable goals, work hard, sacrifice, and
make sound decisions,
I am good enough, just as a human being,
to achieve greatness in life!

Chapter 4

Bob Your Head

I'm tired of writing songs

that depict women, especially black women,

as sluts, whores, and tramps.

I'm tired of writing lyrics that only

degrade females.

I'm tired of talking about

the money in my pocket,

the cars I drive, and the house I live in,

using profanity, and

other foul words,

knowing that most of the people listening to my music

are children.

Now I know why my parents

loved that "old school" music.

Those songs promoted love, affection, and

togetherness.

They were perfect for family reunions!

Men made women out to be beautiful beings.

When those guys wrote and sang songs,

they talked about making up with women.

They used to encourage blacks

to be proud of who they were,

not encourage young black men,

like myself,

to promote ignorance.

My music shows that I really don't care about who's

listening,

yet it does imply that I am very concerned

about the wealth I'm getting.

I'm tired of using profanity,

racial slurs, and other vulgar terms in my songs and

then

having the nerve to thank God for blessing me

with that gift—

for blessing me with an award

that recognizes my talent

to say those rude and disrespectful things.

So what if people buy it?

That does not mean God encouraged them to.

Chapter 5

Taking Advantage

I'm tired of people making exceptions

and excuses for me,

just because I'm the football and basketball star.

I'm tired of my teachers and administrators

letting me get away with breaking the rules

because I'm bringing in revenue for the school

through my football and basketball abilities.

Shouldn't they be more concerned

with what I'm learning in all of my classes, or

if I'm even learning at all?

Shouldn't they at least be a little concerned

with what I'm doing

when I'm not scoring touchdowns, or

making jump shots?

I'm tired of those same people

telling me that they love me, but

their only question to me

is about whether or not our team

is going to win the next game.

They have never asked me

what my plans are

following high school or college.

They don't ask about my interests outside of sports.

Do they care

about me, or

only about

what I can do for their schools and programs?

The university gave me a full scholarship

to pay for my undergraduate education, but

they make millions of dollars every year,

just because

the fans come to see me at the games.

By the way,

my scholarship is only worth $15,000 to $25,000,

per year.

If I'm as good as they say I am,

I'm not going to stay in college four years.

I came from a poor family,

single parent home,

in an inner city neighborhood

with nothing but drugs, prostitution, and

violence around me.

I'm going to run to the worst team in the pros,

when they offer me millions of dollars.

I'll get endorsements from fashion designers and

other companies.

I really don't care that their goal

is to use my name,

to earn money for their company;

far more money

than they will ever pay me.

Then if I accept free "gifts" such as

money, cars, clothes and shoes

from boosters, alumni, or local business owners,

the league is going to fine my school,

and take away our wins, stats, and championships.

The school which supposedly had my back,

will suspend me.

The fans who loved me so much,

are going to talk about how I am a shame and a disgrace

to the name of the institution.

With all of their strict rules and policies,

didn't the league and my school

know that I was ineligible?

They knew where they discovered me and

it wasn't in a mansion.

Why would they let me

play in so many games,

build or help maintain our school's reputation

as an athletic powerhouse, and

draw fans to a venue that was suffering,

just to tell the world I had cheated, taken gifts

I wasn't supposed to, or

violated recruiting guidelines

when they know I'm getting ready

to move on to the professional league?

Keep in mind,

I still haven't learned how to read, proficiently,

or learned how to add, subtract, multiply, or divide.

I don't know how to problem solve or

think critically,

because no one cared

whether or not I possessed those skills.

They only cared about what I could do for them.

Now, they don't need me,

so it's my problem.

Chapter 6

Ignorance

I'm tired of feeling like the only way

I can be viewed as normal

by other black people,

is to show how ignorant I can be.

I'm tired of sagging my pants

because someone lied to me and

told me it was cool.

I'm tired of doing things because they're in style.

I am an individual.

I have the ability

to think for myself.

I'm pretty sure

the same way people influence me,

I can influence

other people.

I'm tired of following trends

instead of starting them.

I'm tired of laughing at my infant and toddler,

sons and daughters, when they use profanity or

repeat foul language

they hear on the radio or on the television.

I'm tired of laughing at them

when they get "smart" or sarcastic

with me or other people.

I'm tired of going to my child's school,

yelling, fussing, and cussing

at their principals, counselors and teachers

when I know my child is wrong.

I'm tired of not caring about my children talking back

to me,

not following my rules,

playing me against their mom,

earning horrible grades in school,

or having sex in my house,

until someone

I'm trying to impress

is present.

I'm tired of their disrespectful behaviors

only frustrating me at funerals, at weddings,

in schools or in grocery stores,

All of a sudden,

I know how to send them to their room,

smack them in the mouth, or

pull out my belt.

I'm tired of their mother not having any control

over them.

She is their parent, as much as I am.

I'm tired of her letting them get away with everything,

but

when they get on her nerves,

embarrass her in public, or

in front of her friends,

she wants to threaten them with,

"I'm going to tell your Daddy."

Chapter 7

Priorities

I'm tired of having my priorities in the wrong order or

not prioritizing the

events and responsibilities in my life, at all.

I'm tired of making entertainment

the last thing I cut from my budget.

If my family stopped bailing me out every time I got

into trouble,

I probably would make better decisions.

I'm tired of asking friends and family members

to help me pay my rent, gas, and water bill

after I just bought tickets

to a concert.

I'm tired of making sure I pay the cable bill,

instead of making sure my family

has food in the refrigerator.

I'm tired of buying my children expensive,

clothes and shoes,

but playing the "poor card"

when they need money for school field trips.

They can do without those

hundred-dollar shoes

if it means they can go to a museum.

Their principal, teachers, or other parents

should not have to bear

that financial burden.

Chapter 8

I Am Who I Am

I'm tired of feeling like I have to buy my children

name-brand clothing and shoes

so they don't get laughed at.

I have seen plenty of children

lag behind the latest fashion, yet

survive school and life,

successfully!

Those children can do it because

they know who they are and

where they come from.

Their parents have given them a sense of

security and identity.

I am responsible

for instilling the same values in my children.

I claim I have raised my children

to feel superior

and proud of who they are, yet

they feel inferior and

wish they were like others.

Security and identity,

are much more affordable

than a pair of tennis shoes

that cost more money than I earn in a day.

Chapter 9

My Fault

I'm tired of making excuses for my failures in life.

My failures in life

are my fault.

The fact that my dad wasn't around

and didn't bother to pay child support—

is not a good enough reason for me to underachieve in

life.

The fact that my family was poor,

doesn't give me the right to have a mediocre life.

If I don't succeed in life,

all of the blame falls on me.

Having a rougher life than others

is an invitation to be a light,

a role model, and

an inspiration to people who come from

a background similar to mine.

Chapter 10

Liking White Women

I'm tired of rejecting the idea of dating white women or

the idea of being married to

a white woman.

I'm tired of being afraid of what my parents or

what my family and friends will say about it.

I'm tired of white women

rejecting me,

because their family and friends

do not approve of black men.

I'm tired of worrying about what people are saying in

public or

how they look at us in public.

Let them stare!

I'm tired of hearing

that I can't go to her home

to meet her parents.

Who cares if her parents don't accept me?

If their reasons are because I'm on drugs,

I beat her, or

I cheat on her,

I totally understand!

However,

if the only reason

they can come up with

is the fact that I'm black,

then it is okay

for her and I to be together.

After all, who is going to be

underneath **OUR** sheets and blankets at night?

Who has to pay **OUR** bills?

Who has to be there for **US**

through the thick and thin?

The only thing that should matter is whether or not

we love each other!

I'm tired of dating white women and

hearing black women say,

"there are only a few good, black men in the world, so

why do white women have to take those?

Why can't they leave those black men for black women?"

Maybe I just don't have a preference

when it comes to color, and

the kind, loving, ambitious,

self-motivated woman

who I am attracted to

just happens to be white.

Why should I be shallow-minded and stuck on color?

I like who I like and

love who I love.

I have the right to date any person I choose and

so does every other man and woman.

Chapter 11

Not Ready for Parenthood

I'm tired of getting females pregnant,

knowing that I am not in a position

to take care of my children.

I'm tired of those same women

allowing me to have unprotected sex with them,

knowing that they can't provide

for our child either.

Besides, there are other risks to consider, such as

sexually transmitted diseases.

We shouldn't be doing it anyway,

but since we are,

one of us

should be responsible enough

to make sure we protect ourselves.

I'm tired of my parents and

grandparents,

taking care of my children,

so that I can party with my friends.

Chapter 12

Useless Assumptions and Stereotypes

I'm tired of the assumptions tied to black men or

black people in general.

I'm tired of women of other races

wanting to be with me

because they heard

black men have "big packages."

Yes, it sounds great and

does tremendous things for my ego, but

when I'm establishing a committed relationship,

that will only be

a small part of the equation.

Sex is only a huge factor for insecure and

immature people.

Guys tend to get caught up in those acknowledgements

more so than women.

A guy can tell a woman about how fine she is,

how big her butt is, or

how nice her breasts are, but

if she is not interested in him, he can forget it.

I'm tired of people thinking that just because I'm black

I want to be greeted as "dog," "son,"

"homey," or "homeboy."

My first thought is,

"you don't know me like that," and

my second thought is,

"Wow! Do people think all black men

want to be approached in that manner?"

I'm tired of people thinking that just because I'm black,

I love fried chicken and watermelon.

I may not like chicken or

might think watermelon is gross.

Get to know me

before you start making assumptions.

Chapter 13

Living a Lie

I'm tired of going to church,

praising the Lord, professing to be a Christian,

being kind to the other members of the church,

as well as the visitors, but

leaving church, and

being mean, rude, and nasty

to my children and spouse.

I'm tired of committing the sins

I preach to others to stay away from, like

fornicating and lying.

I'm tired of using the scriptures in the bible

to justify the wrongful deeds that I do.

I am wrong for using those same scriptures

to get what I want from people

who trust me as their spiritual leader.

Chapter 14

My Vote

I'm tired of voting for black people

just because they're black.

I'm still upset I did it

for President Obama in 2008.

I'm still bothered

that other people didn't vote for him,

just because he's black.

I really don't care what color the president is as

long as he/she provides better treatment for our veterans,

makes education more affordable for students,

ensures quality health care for all citizens and

other people living in the United States.

Throw in a great retirement plan,

guaranteed social security, or at least what I paid into

the program,

and I will support that president, senator, governor, or

mayor.

Chapter 15

Keep Talking

I'm tired of hearing black men

who have an influential voice

in the public,

talking about how young black men

need role models.

Really?

Where did they get that idea from?

It seems like more talking is being done,

than role-modeling.

I'm tired of them only using their voices

after crime in heavily, black populated areas

has gotten out of control.

I'm tired of them only getting in front of television

cameras or

on the radio waves,

when they think they have a case of racial profiling.

Where are their proactive plans?

Where were their mentorship programs yesterday?

Chapter 16

What Civil Rights Movement?

I'm tired of bringing shame to what people like

Martin Luther King, Jr.,

Harriet Tubman and Rosa Parks did for black people.

I'm pretty sure

they didn't fight for blacks to have equal rights and

freedom

for us to steal, rob, and kill each other.

The blacks that came before my generation, and

my parents' generation,

fought for us to have the right to go to school.

Now they have to fight us

to get us to go to school.

They fought for us to have the right to sit

in the front of every establishment.

Now, people have to fight us

to sit in the front of classrooms or

in the front of buses.

The same applies for voting.

It seems to me

that we only wanted rights,

when we didn't have any.

We only wanted to do things

when people said we couldn't.

We were very humble and loving people,

before we had rights.

We can get an education, but

we'd rather be illiterate.

Whites can no longer force us to wear chains

around our necks or wrists, but

we'll go and buy the largest ones

we can find and wear them, freely.

I'm tired of guilt lying within me,

every time I hold a gun to a man's head

and demand his shoes, his money, or

even worse,

his drugs.

When I rob my fellow man,

I'm only showing that I am too lazy

to get a job, or too impatient to save my money,

in order to be able to

purchase the things I want.

Every time I pull a trigger, for someone else's

possessions or

just because it makes me feel good, or

because it makes me look like "the man"

in front of my friends,

I am destroying the works of those

who died, fighting for me to have a better life.

Chapter 17

I Promise, I Can Read

I'm tired of hearing that every,

racial sub-group,

reads more than mine, and

reads more proficiently than mine.

I can read!

I am not illiterate!

I have only reduced myself

to the stereotype

that defines black males.

Ask me what is in the sports section of the newspaper?

I bet I can tell you!

Ask me about cars, whether American, or

foreign?

You can even ask me about car parts,

such as rims.

I bet I can tell you about those too!

I've read a lot about cars in the books and magazines

I checked out from my school's library.

I can read,

I just don't like to read

what I'm told or asked to read.

I don't like to read the dreadful books and stories

my teachers assign.

When I'm forced to read the boring passages on tests,

I just mark any answer,

leaving people to think I can't read.

If some educators were not afraid of lawsuits,

they would hold me to the same standards as the other

children.

Too often, they try to avoid confrontations

with my mother and father, or other black parents,

so they lower their standards for black pupils.

Those that do it,

are not doing us any favors.

They are only setting us up to fail and they are

being unfair to the other students

at the same time.

Chapter 18

Earning a Dollar

I may not want to punch a clock,

knowing that I will only earn minimum wage, but

I promise you,

I can earn a dollar

faster than a teacher,

doctor, lawyer, or businessman.

Give me one bag of weed to sell, and

I'll sell two.

Give me crack to sell, and

I will sell it to your mother

if it'll buy me a Benz.

Just don't ask me to sell insurance, cable, or

soda products.

THAT'S WHACK!

It's like, I can't win,

being black!

Chapter 19

Final Rest

I'm tired of people feeling sorry for me,

rather than trying to help me

work through my personal issues.

Don't feel sorry for me.

Be tough on me; be honest with me.

don't let me down.

Don't refer to me as black, anymore!

After all,

I'm not only black, but I am also human,

and my name is…

Nice to meet you!